DISCOVERING
the Old Stone Age

By Ellen B. Cutler

Editorial Offices: Glenview, Illinois • Parsippany, New Jersey • New York, New York

Sales Offices: Needham, Massachusetts • Duluth, Georgia • Glenview, Illinois
Coppell, Texas • Sacramento, California • Mesa, Arizona

Talking About the Past

History is the written record of human **culture**. History describes the rise and fall of kingdoms, advances in science and art, and changes in religious beliefs. History is full of famous people, but it would not exist without countless individuals whose names are not remembered.

The facts of history come from written records kept by governments, armies, shopkeepers, and homemakers. Any and every document is part of the historical record.

The period of human culture before the invention of writing is called **prehistory**. **Archaeologists** collect **artifacts** left behind by prehistoric peoples, and **anthropologists**, or people who study anthropology, use these artifacts to understand the lives these peoples led. History is about five thousand years old, but prehistory is much, much older.

The story of the past is told through words and objects.

Prehistory and Culture

Determining when prehistory began is more difficult than deciding when it ended. Most scholars agree that prehistory began with human culture. They often disagree, though, about when humans developed culture.

Defining Culture

In anthropology, the word *culture* refers to the shared experiences of a group of people. Part of these experiences is the beliefs and learned knowledge that various group members teach to other group members.

Social attitudes are beliefs. Social beliefs may cause people to treat some members of a family or a village differently from others.

Learned knowledge might include hunting animals or finding plants that are good to eat. Using fire, making tools, and caring for sick or injured individuals are also forms of knowledge. In a culture, knowledge is not only handed down from one generation to the next but is constantly improved.

Finding, growing, and preparing food are all forms of knowledge.

Prehistory Began with Humans

Some scholars say prehistory began about 2 million years ago when our ancestors began to use tools. Still others say that prehistory started about 100,000 years ago when the first modern humans appeared.

There are three ages of prehistory: the Stone Age, the Bronze Age, and the Iron Age. Although scientists disagree as to when each of these ages ended and the next began, it is clear that our prehistory took place almost entirely in the Stone Age.

The Age of Stone

During the Stone Age, humans made tools and personal objects from stone, wood, bones, and shells. Early in the Stone Age, people were **nomads**. They moved from place to place with the seasons, collecting fruits and nuts and hunting animals. Late Stone Age cultures discovered **agriculture**. They began to raise animals, including cows, horses, goats, and dogs, and learned to grow grains and other plants. At the end of the Stone Age, people settled in villages and some of the villages grew into cities.

A bronze axe is an example of an early tool.

The Ages of Metal

Metal **technology** signaled the end of the Stone Age. At the end of the Stone Age, people learned to heat copper ore to get copper metal. During the Bronze Age, people mixed melted copper and tin to create a harder metal called bronze.

The Iron Age followed the Bronze Age. The Iron Age began about 3,000 years ago. Iron was more difficult to work with than bronze, but iron is a stronger metal. Iron tools and weapons were much better than those made of copper and bronze.

Knowledge of metal technology was often passed from one culture to another. Some peoples were introduced to iron without ever having learned about bronze. Some Stone Age cultures survived so long that they jumped directly into the modern era when they came into contact with European explorers.

Writing and the End of Prehistory

Prehistory came to an end at different times as different cultures invented systems of writing. Most cultures developed written language during the Iron Age.

Writing appeared in Egypt and in what is now Iraq about five thousand years ago. Ancient China had a writing system about four thousand years ago. The Aztecs, who lived in Mexico seven hundred years ago, never developed a written language, but they used a system of simple pictures to keep records.

The Sumerians of Mesopotamia
invented a form of wedge-shaped
writing known as cuneiform.

Progress During the Stone Age

The Stone Age lasted about 2.5 million years. During the Stone Age humans spread from the African continent throughout Europe, Asia, and North and South America. Early human cultures invented stone tools, created remarkable works of art, tamed wild animals, and became societies that depended on agriculture.

The Use of Fire

Perhaps the most important "tool" in prehistory was fire. At first, early humans may have taken advantage of small fires caused by lightning. They later figured out how to control these fires and keep them burning. Finally they discovered ways to create fire themselves. Our ancestors were warming themselves with fire about 450,000 years ago.

Fire was important to prehistoric cultures.

A Time Line of Prehistory

3 million years ago   100,000   80,000

The break in the time line means that a part of the time line has been left out. In this case the years between 3 million years ago and 100,000 years ago have been left out of the time line.

Fire gave humans many things. It kept them warm in cold weather and protected them from attacks by wild animals. Cooking made foods taste better, and foods dried in the smoke did not spoil. A crackling fire would have encouraged people to gather together for warmth, safety, and social reasons. Small fires made it possible to work at night and in dark caves.

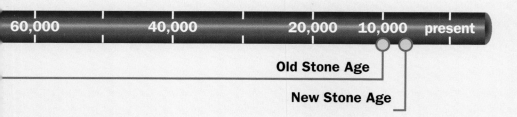

60,000   40,000   20,000   10,000   present

Old Stone Age

New Stone Age

This dagger with a flint blade and a woven pouch were probably used around the New Stone Age.

Prehistoric Artifacts

Early Tools

The oldest artifacts found by archaeologists are made of stone. The first tools—axes, scrapers, and knives—were made from rocks that had been broken to produce a sharp edge. Later Stone Age peoples learned to flake thin pieces from large rocks. These flakes had sharp edges and points. Attached to sticks or long bones, the flakes became arrows and spears or scythes for cutting grasses and grains.

Stone Age peoples shaped tools from bone and antler as well as stone. A variety of points, including spearheads, awls for poking holes in skins, and sewing needles, were made from bone, antler, and ivory.

In addition to paintings, prehistoric people made fine rock carvings, such as this scene that was discovered near Les Eyzies, France.

Prehistoric Art

Carved Objects and Personal Ornaments

Stone Age peoples also left behind works of arts as artifacts. The oldest pieces of prehistoric artwork were small, portable carvings, such as animal and human figures. Personal ornaments made from ivory, shells, and animal teeth were also common. Stone Age artists also decorated weapons and other tools. This made sense for nomads, who were always on the move.

Did these works of art have a purpose or a special meaning? Could ivory beads, for instance, show that the wearer was an important person? Perhaps the figure of an animal served as a good-luck charm. There is no way to know for sure.

Paintings and Wall Decorations

Prehistoric artists decorated caves and stone cliffs with pictures of animals, human figures, and patterns. Red, yellow, and brown colors came from minerals the painters dug from the earth. Black came from burned bones and wood. To make paint the artists ground colors into powder and mixed the powder with water or animal fat. They then dabbed the paint on stone with their fingers or with twigs, or used brushes made from animal hair. They also blew dry, powdered color through hollow bones.

Animals were the most common subjects of their paintings. They painted wild cattle, horses, deer, lions, woolly mammoths, rhinoceros, goats, and other animals. Human figures were rare, but the outlines or prints of human hands were common. Patterns of dots, lines, and spirals were also common.

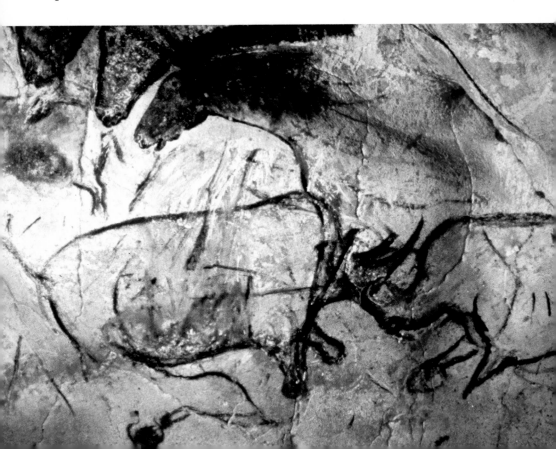

Why create such elaborate decorations in caves? What do the pictures mean?

The purpose and meaning of these paintings are a mystery. The caves would not have been good homes because they are dark, damp, and remote. The pictures themselves are often high up on the walls and very difficult to see.

One theory, or educated guess, is that the pictures were meant to bring about a successful hunt. Many cave paintings show horses, wild cattle, and deer. Prehistoric people hunted all of these animals in great numbers. Other animals that appear in the paintings, such as the rhinoceros, however, were not usually hunted for food. The cave paintings at Chauvet in southern France show at least two separate images of rhinoceros fighting with each other.

Perhaps some animals represented spirits that Stone Age peoples feared or worshipped. Perhaps the caves were used for religious ceremonies.

Some scholars share the theory that the cave paintings are records. According to this theory, the pictures helped people remember important ideas and events. When considered from this point of view, cave paintings are similar to written records.

This cave painting in Chauvet, France, shows images of horses and rhinoceros.

Who Made It . . . and When?

Archaeologists identify artifacts and try to determine when they were made. In order to determine these things, it is important to know exactly where an object was found.

Doing the Dig

The first step in studying artifacts is to collect them. The place where archaeologists find objects is called a dig. Archaeologists describe an excavation site as a dig. A dig is set up so that archaeologists can record exactly where each object was found—how deep in the ground and how near it was to shelters, fireplaces, or other living areas.

The depth at which an artifact was buried tells a lot about its age. The earth is made up of layers of dirt, rock, and other material. Each layer is connected to a particular period of time. An artifact is likely to be the same age as the age of the layer of earth in which it was found.

The archaeologist's next step is to make a map of the area and divide it into small sections called units. Each unit has to be searched slowly and carefully. Some of the surface dirt may be removed with shovels and machines. Much of the dirt, however, is cleared away with brushes and tiny tools. Fast and careless digging may break or scratch precious artifacts. Some artifacts are fairly large and easy to see when they are uncovered. For smaller items, there is a simple but effective process. Some of the dirt is set aside in buckets. This dirt is later put through a screen that lets dirt fall through but holds back bits of stone tools or pieces of bone.

Archaeologists at a dig search slowly and carefully for artifacts.

How old is really old?

Carbon dating is another way to determine the age of an artifact. All living things, both plants and animals, contain the element carbon. One kind of carbon is carbon 14, or C14. As long as a plant or animal is alive, it has C14 inside it. When the plant or animal dies, the C14 starts to disappear. Scientists know that it takes about fifty thousand years for C14 to disappear from a dead plant or animal. If the C14 is all gone, then the object is at least fifty thousand years old. Carbon dating cannot be used on stone. It can, however, be used on paint or animal blood that is stuck to the stone.

If a cave painting, for instance, contains black paint made from burnt wood or bone, a scientist can measure the amount of C14 in the paint. This is how archaeologists decide how old a cave painting might be.

Glossary

agriculture the practice of raising plants or animals for human use

anthropology the study of how people have developed and live in cultural groups

archaeologist a scientist who uncovers evidence, or proof, from the past

artifact an object made by people long ago

carbon dating a method of estimating the age of an animal or a plant after it has died

civilization a group of people who have a complex and organized society within a culture

culture the way in which individuals and groups react with their environment, including their technology, customs, beliefs, and art

nomad a person who travels from place to place without a permanent home

prehistory the long period of time before people developed systems of writing and written language

technology the way in which humans produce the items they use